A CONFIDENT TRUST

In the God You Can Always Count On

70 Uplifting Insights with Scripture

Carol S. Blose

Blessed is the one who trusts in the Lord, whose confidence is in him. They will be like a tree planted by the water that sends out its roots by the stream. It does not fear when heat comes; its leaves are always green. It has no worries in a year of drought and never fails to bear fruit.

—Jeremiah 17:7–8

Contents

Eagle's Wings 

> *They that wait upon the Lord shall renew their strength; they shall mount up with wings of eagles; they shall run, and not be weary; and they shall walk and not faint.*
>
> —Isaiah 40:31 KJV

The eagle uses gusts of wind underneath its body to propel it forward—riding on the wind, gliding, and soaring through the air with great ease. It uses its wingspan to bring balance arriving at its destination effortlessly. A baby eagle begins to fly by hopping around the nest first then to nearby branches, gaining strength and balance as it grows. The baby eagle will then leap from the branch, taking flight for the first time.

Like the baby eagle, there are always first-time experiences that need to happen in life. There are times when you need to jump into an area that is unknown to you and learn from it because it will create growth. Taking risks is part of life that can look scary at times because it requires you to get out of your comfort zone.

In the kingdom of God, growing spiritually is a process. Jesus wants to give you a new understanding in the Word of God that will bring revelation of who He is. He desires to have daily conversations to discuss all that you're pondering in your heart. He longs to bring you freedom from fear that might hinder your growth and hold you back. And like that eagle, begin by taking small steps as you learn to trust Him. Then hop off that place that is very familiar, jumping forward into something new, and begin to soar with the King of kings!

> For God did not give us a spirit of fear, but of power, love and of a sound mind. (2 Timothy 1:7 NIV)

Have I not commanded you? Be strong and courageous. Do not be afraid, do not be discouraged, for the LORD your God will be with you wherever you go. (Joshua 1:9 NIV)

Purity and Beauty

> *See, I am doing a new thing! Now it springs up; do*
> *you not perceive it? I am making a way in the wil-*
> *derness and streams in the wasteland.*
>
> —Isaiah 43:19 NIV

When going through a difficult season in life, it's good to have a different perspective that can influence your viewpoint. For instance, when looking out a window in the desert, you're likely to see brown sand, rocks, and cactus. However, when a large white crane suddenly flies into view and lands on one of the rocks to sun himself, the scene immediately changes. The brown scene that you've been looking at has now shifted, adding beauty and movement in the midst of the ordinary.

The Lord wants to give you a heavenly perspective when viewing the scenes in your life. To be able to see circumstances as He sees them. He longs to bring refreshment to you when you find yourself in that dry desert place. In the mundane moments of daily living, Jesus can bring wisdom and revelation to you when you ask Him.

God has so much more for you than just a brown backdrop. Allow the purity and beauty of the Holy Spirit to rule in your heart, for He is always good. As you come closer to God, abiding and trusting in Him, you'll find yourself stepping into His heavenly oasis as you begin to gaze on the beauty of who He is.

> One thing I ask from the Lord, this only do I
> seek: that I may dwell in the house of the Lord
> all the days of my life, to gaze on the beauty of
> the Lord and to seek him in his temple. (Psalm
> 27:4 NIV)

I keep asking that the God of our Lord Jesus
Christ, the glorious Father, may give you the
Spirit of wisdom and revelation, so that you may
know him better. (Ephesians 1:17 NIV)

Strategic Moves 

> *I will instruct you and teach you in the way you should*
> *go; I will counsel you with my loving eye on you.*
> —Psalm 32:8 NIV

Now there are times when you might find yourself at a crossroad in life. Like a game of strategy, it's a place where options come into play. You can come to a crossroad in your business that requires you to relocate your family to another state in order to grow. There are also times of grief and loss that can bring you to a crossroad.

The changes that you face and choices that need to be made moving ahead are not always black and white. There are times when any change seems overwhelming, and fear begins to set in because you're not sure that the direction you choose will be the right one. Remember that you are never alone as God is always with you. He wants to be a part of everything you do in life including every change you make.

Come before the Lord, seek Him in prayer, and trust in Him. He will give you wisdom, a plan of action, and strategic moves that will put you on the right path. God loves you and values you. He knows which road is the right one that will bring you fulfillment. Do not move ahead of God, but allow Him to be the strategist that leads you by His Spirit with peace.

> Whether you turn to the right or to the left, your
> ears will hear a voice behind you, saying, "This is
> the way; walk in it." (Isaiah 30:21 NIV)

> Trust in the Lord with all your heart and lean not
> on your own understanding; in all your ways sub-
> mit to him, and he will make your paths straight.
> (Proverbs 3:5–6 NIV)

Realignment

> *Do not be anxious about anything, but in every situation, by prayer and petition, with thanksgiving, present your requests to God. And the peace of God, which transcends all understanding, will guard your hearts and your minds in Christ Jesus.*
>
> —Philippians 4:6–7 NIV

You've most likely experienced a time in your life where your alarm clock didn't go off, so you overslept; you're running to get out the door and even skipped your morning cup of coffee! On your way to work, you're driving faster on the freeway than you usually do. Suddenly, you're seeing red brake lights on the cars in front of you, and traffic is slowing down rapidly. You are now starting to panic as you have a few miles to go before you reach your destination. You begin to think of the meeting that you cannot be late for, and anxiety starts to overwhelm your mind and heart.

When you encounter a situation that is not expected, throws off your routine, or is out of your control, take a deep breath and speak the name of Jesus. Allow the Holy Spirit to bring a calmness to your heart, knowing that you cannot accomplish anything by allowing anxiety to rule over you.

Steer clear of frustration and stress by allowing God to realign your mind and heart and bring you peace when you need it most. He is your refuge and strong tower. Put your trust in Jesus as His love for you endures forever.

Let the peace of Christ rule in your hearts, since as members of one body you were called to peace. And be thankful. (Colossians 3:15 NIV)

Give thanks to the LORD, for he is good. His love endures forever. (Psalm 136:1 NIV)

Unique

I praise you, because I am fearfully and wonderfully made; your works are wonderful, I know that full well.

—Psalm 139:14 NIV

People today seem to compare with one another all kinds of things. Clothes and hairstyles to the best smartphone, the nicest home, who is the most attractive, has the ideal career, the highest income to the most likes and followers on social media, and the list goes on.

God created each person unique and different. His desire was not that all people be identical but that each person He created have individual interests, gifts, talents, and distinct personalities. That way, when you come together, you will have much to offer each other as well as to the world you live in. Look at each other through the eyes of a loving God. Honoring one another's promotions and victories, mourning together when one is suffering, and giving support when a helping hand is needed.

God is not a respecter of persons and does not show partiality. Do not let what you think you lack be a focal point. When God looks upon you, He sees a diverse individual, created in His image and likeness. You have an incomparable purpose in God's kingdom. You are very valuable, highly-favored, and God celebrates your uniqueness!

So that there should be no division in the body, but that its parts should have equal concern for each other. If one part suffers, every part suffers with it; if one part is honored, every part rejoices with it. (1 Corinthians 12:25–26 NIV)

Then Peter began to speak: I now realize how
true it is that God does not show favoritism.
(Acts 10:34 NIV)

9

Puzzle Pieces

In their hearts, humans plan their course, but the Lord establishes their steps.

—Proverbs 16:9 NIV

When putting a puzzle together, you want to find all the pieces that fit together perfectly, so when the puzzle is finished, you'll have a complete and beautiful picture! Have you ever seen a puzzle piece that looked like the right piece because it had a similar shape and the right colors, but when you tried to put it where you thought it would go, it wouldn't quite fit?

Perhaps there are times when you find yourself trying to control or force things to happen when you don't see the Lord moving quite as fast as you'd like Him to. You've neglected to invite God into your situation in a certain area of your life because you've already decided how you want things to go. However, when you're trying to make something happen that God is not calling you to, or is not God's timing, you might find that the circumstances don't quite fit or feel right.

God knows what's always best for you. However, your thoughts can take you to a place that believes God will lead you in the direction you don't want to go. Instead of trying to make things happen, put your trust in Him and seek the Lord for His direction and timing. Allow God to put the pieces of your life together in such a way that it creates peace and harmony. Because when the time is right, it will be a perfect fit!

> Whenever my busy thoughts were out of control,
> the soothing comfort of your presence calmed
> me down and overwhelmed me with delight.
> (Psalm 94:19 TPT)

Trust in the Lord with all your heart and lean not
on your own understanding; in all your ways submit to him, and he will make your paths straight.
(Proverbs 3:5–6 NIV)

Priceless Treasure

> *My help comes from the LORD, the Maker of heaven and earth. He will not let your foot slip— he who watches over you will not slumber; indeed, he who watches over Israel will neither slumber nor sleep.*
>
> *—Psalm 121:2–4 NIV*

God knows there are occasional days and nights when you feel sadness, discouragement, or disappointment and times when you don't feel appreciated. God is aware of what your mind is focused on and what thoughts are keeping you awake at night. During times of overthinking and sleeplessness, draw near to God, and He will pour out His healing balm over your mind and heart and give you rest.

The Lord wants you to know that He is a close father, and He always has time for you. He never slumbers or sleeps, and He loves you unconditionally. However, in this life, there will be people you care about that will fall short and let you down. Release them to God and forgive them as He has forgiven you.

You are God's most valuable treasure. Do not look at yourself as you perceive others might see you: as a trinket that is easily replaced. See yourself as God sees you: a priceless treasure shining brightly that He longs to commune with for an eternity, for He cherishes you.

> The LORD hath appeared of old unto me, saying,
> Yea, I have loved thee with an everlasting love:
> therefore with lovingkindness have I drawn thee.
> (Jeremiah 31:3 KJV)

Come to me, all you who are weary and burdened, and I will give you rest. Take my yoke
upon you and learn from me, for I am gentle and
humble in heart, and you will find rest for your
souls. (Matthew 11:28–29 NIV)

Uncontained 

Now to him who is able to do immeasurably more than all we ask or imagine, according to his power that is at work within us, to him be the glory in the church and in Christ Jesus throughout all generations, forever and ever! Amen.

> —Ephesians 3:20–21 NIV

Many people try to put God in a box because they cannot fathom His vastness and His glorious majesty. They try to mold an infinite God into a form of human understanding. God has unlimited power and wisdom, and He is not limited by space or time and cannot be contained by preconceived ideas one might have about Him.

Have you ever felt that your plan for the future might differ from God's will for your life? Do you allow your beliefs to be defined by your own plans and preferences instead of God's? God's plan for your life is always good, and His ways will be better than what you can imagine.

As you trust in Him, allow your life to be led by the Holy Spirit, eliminating any preconceived ideas you've had about Him. Surrender to Him as His supernatural wisdom and knowledge far outshines your own understanding about your life and the direction it's taking. God's amazing goodness toward you will always exceed your expectations!

For my thoughts are not your thoughts, neither are your ways my ways, declares the Lord. As the heavens are higher than the earth, so are my ways higher than your ways and my thoughts than your thoughts. (Isaiah 55:8–9 NIV)

I am the Alpha and Omega, the First and the Last, the Beginning and the End. (Revelation 22:13 NIV)

Fragrant Bouquets

*So then, just as you received Christ Jesus as Lord,
continue to live your lives in him, rooted and built
up in him, strengthened in the faith as you were
taught, and overflowing with thankfulness.*
—Colossians 2:6–7 NIV

When starting a flower garden, you plant seeds or small plants of your choice into healthy soil. They soon take root, and with proper sunlight and water, they begin to grow. In their appointed time and season, they can become fragrant bouquets in full bloom. They bring a diversity of color and beauty to the outside as well as the inside of your home.

As you grow spiritually, there are similarities to beautiful flowers in full bloom. God has created you to open up in astounding color as you display the gifts He has given to you for the benefit of expanding God's kingdom. When becoming rooted and grounded in God, your roots go deep in the Word of God. Your understanding of who He is and in knowing how much he loves you begins to blossom.

Enjoy God's abiding presence in every appointed time and season as the Son's light is never extinguished. As you stay close to Him, you will continue to grow, become fragrant, and flourish, and you will bring unforgettable beauty to those around you!

> The righteous will flourish like a palm tree, they will grow like a cedar of Lebanon; planted in the house of the LORD, they will flourish in the courts of our God. (Psalm 92:12–13 NIV)

> And so we know and rely on the love God has for us. God is love. Whoever lives in love lives in God, and God in them. (1 John 4:16 NIV)

Projecting Lies

> *We are destroying sophisticated arguments and every exalted and proud thing that sets itself up against the [true] knowledge of God, and we are taking every thought and purpose captive to the obedience of Christ.*
>
> —2 Corinthians 10:5 AMP

Satan is an enemy that wants to project lies and negative thoughts into your mind and then attempts to magnify them until you find yourself thinking about them all the time. They can possibly be thoughts of anger over what someone said or did, thoughts of fear, insecurity, or unworthiness, to name a few. God does not want you to have an ongoing negative thought life, to live with fear, or to come into agreement with any lies from the enemy.

Satan is the father of lies, and his plan is to steal, kill, and destroy, but *God has come that you may have life and have it to the full.* When you find yourself in a negative thinking pattern because the enemy is projecting his lies, call upon Jesus. He has given you authority over the enemy to take *every thought captive to the obedience of Christ,* bringing freedom.

You have the ability to control what you think about. Don't ponder thoughts that keep you in a prolonged place of fear or anger, but instead, take every thought captive to the obedience of Christ. Your thoughts will become life-giving, peaceful, and joyous!

> Now the Lord is the Spirit, and where the Spirit of the Lord is, there is freedom. (2 Corinthians 3:17 NIV)

The thief comes only to steal and kill and destroy;
I have come that they may have life, and have it
to the full. (John 10:10 NIV)

Shelf Life

*I will cry to God Most High, who accomplishes all
things on my behalf [for He completes my purpose
in His plan].*

—Psalm 57:2 AMP

Doll collectors love collecting different types of dolls—baby dolls, antique dolls, Barbie dolls, talking dolls, and current trendy dolls too. But what do dolls do? They sit on a shelf until someone takes them down and uses them as they were meant to be used, depending on what type of doll it is.

Do you ever feel like you're sitting on a shelf in life not being used by God as He intended? Jesus has a plan for each of His children. Call on Him, and He will guide you. He knows the season you're in and in what direction you should be headed. He will open doors of opportunity and bring the connections you need to go forward and the boldness to take the path you are meant to walk.

Anticipate and trust what God will do and where He wants to take you. Don't discount opportunities that come your way because they are unfamiliar to you as they may be a blessing in disguise. Begin a new adventure and jump off the shelf and follow Jesus!

> But I have raised you up for this very purpose,
> that I might show you my power and that my
> name might be proclaimed in all the earth.
> (Exodus 9:16 NIV)

> Many are the plans in a person's heart, but it is
> the Lord's purpose that prevails. (Proverbs 19:21
> NIV)

Bringing Up the Sun 

When the sun begins to go down and you're watching a beautiful sunset, you know that your day is coming to an end. You have come to trust that the sun will come up and shine again at the perfect time the next day and every other day. You also believe that the birds will be singing and chirping in the early morning hours as well as roosters crowing to welcome the beginning of a new day.

There are things that God has created by His hand that you've trusted in every day and taken for granted. God has never missed bringing up the sun at the appointed time each day. Why is it so difficult at times to trust that He can bring provision for some of the challenges you face in life?

There is nothing on this earth that God cannot provide for. Your needs are not a problem for the King of kings and Lord of lords. Come before Him in prayer; put your trust in Him, and walk in the joy of the Lord knowing that He goes before and behind you. He desires to meet every need, fill your day with peace, and continue to bring the early morning songbirds to greet you each morning!

> The Lord is my strength and my shield; my heart trusts in him, and he helps me. My heart leaps for joy, and with my song I praise him. (Psalm 28:7 NIV)

> And my God will meet all your needs according to the riches of his glory in Christ Jesus. (Philippians 4:19 NIV)

True Identity

> *You are a chosen people, a royal priesthood, a holy nation, God's special possession, that you may declare the praises of him who called you out of darkness into his wonderful light.*
> —1 Peter 2:9 NIV

When attending a costume party, a mask covers one's true identity, and people see an image that is not who they really are. Sometimes, people wear masks in life as a disguise. They might give the impression that they are always confident, although what they are really feeling inside is doubt and uncertainty. Wearing a mask can be a protection, believing if others do not see how they truly feel, they will not face rejection.

God wants you to reflect on your true identity of who you are in Him. He does not have a limited earthly perception of who you are. He sees far beyond how you see yourself and your human weaknesses that you focus on. God loves you, and He wants you to reflect the confidence that results from your relationship with Him. Do not dwell in the poverty of the enemy's lies that say you're not enough, for you are created in the image of God.

Take off that mask and come into alignment with God as he changes your earthly mindset to having a heavenly perception of yourself. Your true identity is in Christ, and you are beautiful in His sight!

> Therefore, if anyone is in Christ, the new creation has come: The old has gone, the new is here! (2 Corinthians 5:17 NIV)

So God created mankind in his own image, in the image of God he created them; male and female he created them. (Genesis 1:27 NIV)

Refreshment and Renewal 

He makes me lie down in green pastures, he leads me
beside quiet waters, he refreshes my soul. He guides
me along the right paths for his name's sake.
                                    —Psalm 23:2–4 NIV

God knows that your life can be busy, and there are so many things competing for your time each day. The Lord sees you text your friends, family, and fellow workers communicating your plans. He sees all the busy thoughts that are going through your mind as the day progresses. You wonder if you will have enough hours in the day to accomplish everything you have on your list of things to do.

As you choose to make time for God in your daily life and put Him first, He will bring balance to your life. He will pour His love and peace over your mind and heart filling you with His presence. As you listen to His voice, let your time together be a time of sweet communion, refreshment, and renewal.

As you begin to walk in the fullness of God, you can confidently face the people you interact with. You will handle the tasks in front of you at work, at home, or wherever you are with a peaceful heart and with much wisdom. There's no need to dread what you might face during the week ahead knowing that Jesus goes before you. Allow God to direct your steps, renew your strength, and bring you peace, refreshment, and joy!

> But those who hope in the Lord will renew their
> strength. They will soar on wings like eagles; they
> will run and not grow weary, they will walk and
> not be faint. (Isaiah 40:31 NIV)

> The Lord makes firm the steps of the one who
> delights in him. (Psalm 37:23 NIV)

Unclear Ahead

God is always with you in times of darkness and trial when things look unclear ahead of you and when you don't understand why a certain situation is happening in your life. Although some time has passed, God has not forgotten you even though it may appear to you that He has. Through unresolved circumstances, can you trust in the Lord even though things do not seem to be working out in your timing or in the way you would like to see them? Can you believe that God's purposes are always at work in your life and what the enemy meant for evil, God can turn it around for good?

Keep your thoughts focused on Him, not what is reeling around in your mind. Sit before the Lord and speak to Him about the details of what concerns you. Know that God hears your every word, and He does not lack understanding. Do not spend countless hours wondering why certain things have happened or what others might think. God is your rock, your hiding place, your refuge, and your deliverer.

You can be confident that God will never leave or forsake you. You may not always understand His ways, but continue to trust Him. When your heart is focused on Him, allow God's peace to pour over you in times of conflict, keeping a spirt of hope and joy as you wait on Him.

> The name of the Lord is a fortified tower; the righteous run to it and are safe. (Proverbs 18:10 NIV)

> And the peace of God, which transcends all understanding, will guard your hearts and your minds in Christ Jesus. (Philippians 4:7 NIV)

Soaring

Hang gliding is not only an opportunity to see beautiful scenery that surrounds you, but there is a sense of complete freedom and a feeling of exhilaration as you soar through the sky. Before you launch from solid ground into the air for the first time, you must be willing to take a risk and trust that the hang glider with its light frame will not fall apart in the air and that you will be able to land on the ground safely without injury.

When you feel God is asking you to do something that you are unfamiliar with, are you willing to take a risk, go out of your comfort zone, and trust Him? Whatever God asks you to do, He will always equip you to do. As you begin to step forward in obedience to Him, He goes before you, and He will not let you fall.

You can reach new spiritual heights in your life when you are willing to follow Jesus. Like hang gliding, take a risk and let your spirit take flight, and soar with Him. God has much joy and freedom ahead that He longs for you to experience!

Now may the God of peace who through the blood of the eternal covenant brought back from the dead our Lord Jesus, that great Shepherd of the sheep, equip you with everything good for doing his will, and may he work in us what is pleasing to him, through Jesus Christ, to whom be glory forever and ever. Amen. (Hebrews 13:20–21 NIV)

For with God nothing shall be impossible. (Luke 1:37 KJV)

God's Remodel

He provided redemption for his people; he ordained his covenant forever—holy and awesome is His name.

—Psalm 111:9 NIV

Now there are shows on television that demonstrate flipping a house that's in great need of repair. They might start by creating the rooms in the house to have better flow and perhaps enlarging rooms by taking down certain walls. The kitchen and bathrooms get updated using beautiful finishes to make what once was thought to be beyond fixing like new again.

There are people in life that have experienced a hurtful past which has eaten away at their confidence and has stolen their identity of who God created them to be. Like termites of the enemy, their walls of stability start to fall. Perhaps some feel they have made too many bad choices in their life that are beyond God's forgiveness. No one is out of God's reach. God is always willing to forgive, heal, redeem, and restore.

Whatever you may have been through in your life so far does not define you. God sees those that have sinned against you and sees how you might have sinned against others. God has immeasurable compassion, and His forgiveness, mercy, and healing doesn't run out. It's His desire to bring restoration to your life. Look to Jesus, for He's not only your Savior and Lord, but He can make what was thought to be beyond repair like new again!

I have swept away your offenses like a cloud, your sins like the morning mist. Return to me, for I have redeemed you. (Isaiah 44:22 NIV)

The thief comes only to steal and kill and destroy;
I have come that they may have life, and have it
to the full. (John 10:10 NIV)

Spiritual Glasses

> *Indeed, if you call out for insight and cry aloud for understanding, and if you look for it as for silver and search for it as for hidden treasure, then you will understand the fear of the LORD and find the knowledge of God.*
>
> —Proverbs 2:3–5 NIV

Do you have your spiritual eyes open? You can see many things with your natural eyes that God gave you. However, you can also see with spiritual sight that comes from the Holy Spirit. Like multifocal contact lenses that help you see clearly at all distances, God can give you spiritual lenses that can help you see and discern the near and the far.

God's vision is always perfect. When you ask God to illuminate your spiritual vision showing you what He wants you to see, it might be like seeing a huge billboard sign on the side of the road that gets your attention. He might bring a picture or a word to your mind that brings you discernment in your circumstance.

You might experience tunnel vision if you're focusing on a particular issue and trying to handle it in your own strength. Invite God into your situation and ask Him to give you spiritual eyes to see, and you will begin to see the light at the end of the tunnel. Trust that God will give you the discernment and understanding that's needed to stop any confusion. It's never God's intention to leave you in the dark, but to give you the clear vision that you've been searching for.

> And this is my prayer; that your love may abound more and more in knowledge and depth of insight, so that you may be able to discern what is best and may be pure and blameless for the day of Christ. (Philippians 1:9–10 NIV)

For God is not the author of confusion, but of peace, as in all churches of the saints. (1 Corinthians 14:33 NIV)

Family

The Lord sees the challenges that one can face with family members at times. Continued arguing and differences of opinion that cause anger and hurt along with anxiety-filled days. Family issues can take away your peace as your thoughts are consumed with wondering how to make the situation better. God knows that this conflict is causing emotional fatigue, but don't lose hope or let discouragement take hold.

As God loves you, He also loves those that are closest to you. When you start to feel tension building in the room, be aware of His presence with you. Ask for God's peace to cover you and to fill your mouth with words of wisdom. A soft answer will turn away wrath. Try to see each one of your family members the way He sees them: as beloved children. Treat them better than they deserve even when it's difficult. Yes, they have flaws as all people on this earth do, but God has given you what you need to extend grace and mercy.

Be generous with forgiveness, love, and mercy. Surrender anything you might be carrying against them to Jesus. When you do this, they will begin to respond in a positive way to your kindness and goodness toward them, bringing God's peace and harmony back to you and your family.

> Bear with each other and forgive one another
> if any of you has a grievance against someone.
> Forgive as the Lord forgave you. (Colossians 3:13
> NIV)

A new command I give you: Love one another. As
I have loved you, so you must love one another.
(John 13:34 NIV)

Earthen Vessel

*Yet you, LORD, are our Father. We are the clay, you
are the potter; we are all the work of your hand.*
—Isaiah 64:8 NIV

God is the potter, and you are the clay. He is in the process of shaping you into a beautiful earthen vessel to be used for His glory and purposes. Some of God's vessels that are shaped by His hand are like water pitchers; they pour cool water over those that are thirsty and in need of refreshing. There are others that are shaped as a cup that is filled with a tasty hot beverage offering hospitality and conversation to those that need a friend. Others are shaped like a tall vase and act as God's arms that are wrapped around those that need to be held and comforted.

God has shaped you into the vessel that is best suited for you with the gifts He has given to you. Although your clay is weak on its own, His refining fire will strengthen you. After you have been tested by fire, you will come forth as a beautiful and useful vessel that is not easily broken.

As you begin to go where God leads you, He will bring those divine opportunities your way. As your fortified vessel reflects His heart, He will use you for His glory and purposes!

> This third I will put into the fire; I will refine them like silver and test them like gold. They will call on my name and I will answer them; I will say, "They are my people," and they will say, "The LORD is our God." (Zechariah 13:9 NIV)

Go down to the potter's house, and there I will give you my message. So I went down to the potter's house, and I saw him working at the wheel. But the pot he was shaping from the clay was marred in his hands; so the potter formed it into another pot, shaping it as seemed best to him. (Jeremiah 18: 2–4 NIV)

Hiding Place 

> *The righteous cry out, and the Lord hears them; he delivers them from all their troubles. The Lord is close to the brokenhearted and saves those who are crushed in spirit. The righteous person may have troubles, but the Lord delivers him from them all.*
> —Psalm 34:17–19 NIV

Life can become overwhelming at times if circumstances in front of you appear hopeless and unsolvable. One can experience a range of emotions including disillusionment, depression, despair, or broken-hearted if faced with trouble in a marriage or career, grieving the loss of a loved one, or dealing with health problems.

God is your hiding place—a very present help in times of trouble and pain. Take refuge in Him knowing that He knows exactly what you're feeling and what you need. You don't need to fear, for the Lord says that He will never leave or forsake you. Call out to God and seek His presence, and He will bring encouragement and comfort to your heart.

Like a searchlight, His beacon shines upon you even when you're going through the darkest of nights. He will guide you in the direction you should go day by day and step-by-step. He will bring you through the darkness that surrounds you. He will sing over you and bring you peace, rest, and hope.

> You are my hiding place; you will protect me from trouble and surround me with songs of deliverance. (Psalm 32:7 NIV)

I called on your name, Lord, from the depths of the pit. You heard my plea: "Do not close your ears to my cry for relief." You came near when I called you, and you said, "Do not fear." (Lamentations 3:55–57 NIV)

Heavenly Perspective 

He determines the number of the stars and calls
them each by name.
—Psalm 147:4 NIV

The night sky can appear so dark and still, but when you look up and see the stars that God has created against the dark sky, it begins to come alive with light and expression. As the stars appear to twinkle, you appreciate their beauty as God has placed them in the sky for your enjoyment, and He knows each one by name. As you look up at the stars, they appear to be small because they are so far away. Think about what it might be like if you were closer to one of those stars. The closer you got, the larger and brighter it would become.

In your personal times of stillness, God wants you to see Him from a higher and heavenly perspective. His love for you is so much bigger than you can possibly imagine, and He is so much greater than your human understanding can fathom. Focus on the Lord as He wants you to see Him up close. Look intently into His face and behold his beauty that you have not yet experienced.

Like those stars, many of God's children see Him from a distance. They have only seen a glimpse of God's glory. He longs for you to see and know so much more of who He is. Lift up your eyes, gaze upon Him, and let Jesus reveal His brilliance and majesty to you up close!

> When I consider your heavens, the work of your fingers, the moon and the stars, which you have set in place, what is mankind that you are mindful of them, human beings that you care for them? You have made them a little lower than the angels and crowned them with glory and honor. (Psalm 8:3–5 NIV)

The heavens declare the glory of God, the skies
proclaim the work of his hands. (Psalm 19:1
NIV)

Riding on God's Power 

—Isaiah 30:21 NIV

When you see a herd of horses running together, they are not only beautiful but also they are strong and powerful animals that have been a part of every generation. They have been a part of war and of celebration, dressed and decorated in a parade or circus with thousands of people watching and cheering. Horses have carried kings and princesses, expert riders, ordinary men, women, and children of all ages on their backs.

Although horses are led with a bit and bridle giving them direction, God doesn't want to lead you that way, leaving you without a choice. He desires to lead you by the power of the Holy Spirit if you choose to be led by Him. Riding on God's strength and power will always sustain you over rough terrain, hills, and valleys that you might experience through the circumstances that you face.

You will be unafraid and secure knowing He is with you wherever you go. God's timing is always perfect in every situation, and you can depend on Him to carry you to your destination.

> Teach me to do your will, for you are my God;
> may your good Spirit lead me on level ground.
> (Psalm 143:10 NIV)

> For all who are allowing themselves to be led by
> the Spirit of God are sons of God. (Romans 8:14
> AMP)

Unseen Prisons

Just as there are many people in physical prisons that are paying a price for the crime they have committed in this life, there are also many that live in prisons that are unseen. Even though they are physically free, they are bound by the lies of the enemy through an unwillingness to forgive. The one that walks in bitterness and unforgiveness is bound by prison bars of the heart.

Our God is a God of unending love, compassion, and mercy. He longs for all his children to walk in total freedom, not bound by invisible bars that keep their heart locked up. Be willing to let go of any past hurts. God has forgiven you of many sins; likewise, forgive those that have sinned against you.

When you're willing to forgive, the chains will begin to fall off, setting you free by the power of the Holy Spirit. Peace and joy that God desires for you will fill your heart. You will experience a lightness of heart that is not weighed down knowing that true freedom is only possible through Jesus!

> Be kind and helpful to one another, tenderhearted [compassionate, understanding], forgiving one another [readily and freely], just as God in Christ also forgave you. (Ephesians 4:32 AMP)

> So if the Son sets you free, you will be free indeed. (John 8:36 NIV)

Rain

—Isaiah 45:8 NIV

God created the rain to replenish the earth. When flowers in bloom begin to wilt, a light, refreshing rain will perk them up again. There are times when your life gets busy, and before you know it, weeks have passed, and you haven't connected with the Lord. As you find yourself beginning to wilt spiritually, call on the name of Jesus, and He will shower you with a refreshing rain of His Spirit. Refocus your attention on God once again allowing Him to revive and energize you.

There are also times when the earth needs a heavy or cleansing rain. The air can become polluted; however, a heavy rain cleans up the atmosphere so that you can see the majestic mountaintops from afar. Your life can also become polluted by the world since you live with ungodliness all around you. Allow the cleansing rain of God's Spirit to wash off the negative effects of the world that pollutes your mind and heart. You'll then be able to see circumstances clearly from God's perspective.

God's abundant rain can fall on the earth for days at a time, and rivers, lakes, and waterways are replenished. When your heart is in a spiritual drought, come before the Lord and let Him pour out His abundant rain over your life. A downpour of God's Spirit that is overflowing with blessings will fill your heart with praise, love, hope, and joy!

He says to the snow, "Fall on the earth," and to the rain shower, "Be a mighty downpour." (Job 37:6 NIV)

May the God of hope fill you with all joy and peace as you trust in him, so that you may overflow with hope by the power of the Holy Spirit. (Romans 15:13 NIV)

Strengthened and Chosen 

> *So do not fear, for I am with you; do not be dismayed, for I am your God. I will strengthen you and help you; I will uphold you with my righteous right hand.*
>
> —Isaiah 41:10 NIV

If a dam is old and hasn't had the updated repairs that's needed, it can weaken to the point of breaking. There can be a lot of damage and possible lives lost as a result. There is a rebuilding that will need to take place to make it stronger than before, so it will not weaken over time.

There are times when some rebuilding or changes in one's thinking need to take place, especially when those thoughts don't come into agreement with God's Word. If you see yourself as unworthy or walk in guilt or shame, adjustments in your thoughts need to be made according to who God says you are. When God looks at you, He sees the righteousness of Jesus because when you received Jesus as your savior, you became a new creation in Christ.

Don't let the enemy bring doubt of who you are in God and weaken how you see yourself. God wants to strengthen those places in your heart that need rebuilding with a godly mindset. If you sin, ask for forgiveness, and keep walking forward with Him hand in hand. Hold your head high because you are a chosen child of the Most High God!

> Therefore, if anyone is in Christ, the new creation has come: The old has gone, the new is here! (2 Corinthians 5:17 NIV)

For you are a people holy to the Lord your God. The Lord your God has chosen you out of all the people on the face of the earth to be his people, his treasured possession. (Deuteronomy 7:6 NIV)

Growth in the Darkness 

Having been deeply rooted [in Him] and now being continually built up in Him and [becoming increasingly more] established in your faith, just as you were taught, and overflowing in it with gratitude.
—Colossians 2:7 AMP

There's a time of watering and allowing the sun to nourish a seed that has been planted in the soil. There's also a time of waiting before you see that little sprout of life spring up. What's not revealed to you is what's happening beneath the soil. There is a process of growth that's taking place in the darkness.

Like that seed that's planted in the soil, there are times when you need to wait on God to work in areas of your life that you cannot see. God is always working, although you might not recognize it. Do not fixate on what you feel is not happening, but keep your focus on Him as He knows what you need, and His timing is perfect.

God can give you hope, joy, and peace even in a time of waiting. You'll notice that little sprout of life begins to spring up within your heart as God is continually accomplishing His work in you. As you remain in Jesus, your faith continues to grow as you stay grounded and rooted in Him. Give God thanks for all that He's doing and will continue to do in your life.

I am the vine; you are the branches. If you remain in me and I in you, you will bear much fruit; apart from me you can do nothing. (John 15:5 NIV)

Planted in the house of the LORD, They will flourish in the courts of our God. (Psalm 92:13 AMP)

Intricately Designed

So God created the great creatures of the sea and every living thing with which the water teems and that moves about in it, according to their kinds, and every winged bird according to its kind. And God saw that it was good.

—Genesis 1:21 NIV

The beaches that God has created all over the world are not only beautiful, but their waves are refreshing as they wash over you. God has created the waves to continually crash onto the shore, and they are lovely to watch and to listen to their distinctive and relaxing sound. God has also created a vast aquarium teeming with life and beauty under countless miles of ocean.

When you think about the myriad of fish that He has created—from microscopic sea creatures to large mammals such as whales and dolphins to an array of colorful corals that live under the sea—you will find that each of them are intricately designed. Each one has its own unique color, texture, and shape. What God creates, regardless of its size, is not random, but carefully thought out.

You are a child of God, and His thoughts toward you are so much greater than the width and depth of the ocean. He has created you with special gifts and talents. You are unique, and there is no one just like you. Your life is not by chance but is fashioned by God's hand, for you are delightful and precious to Him!

I praise you because I am fearfully and wonderfully made; your works are wonderful, I know that full well. (Psalm 139:14 NIV)

We have different gifts, according to the grace given to each of us. If your gift is prophesying, then prophesy in accordance with your faith; if it is serving, then serve; if it is teaching, then teach; if it is to encourage, then give encouragement; if it is giving, then give generously; if it is to lead, do it diligently; if it is to show mercy, do it cheerfully. (Romans 12:6–8 NIV)

Two-Way Street

As you're traveling in your car thinking about the next thing you need to do today, know that God is with you. He would like to have a personal two-way conversation discussing all that's on your mind. If you have any anxiety about your meeting later at work today or have any concerns about that much needed talk with a family member tonight, He desires to give you wisdom and counsel.

Life can get busy, overwhelming at times, and while you're in your fast-paced lane of life, slow down and take a few minutes and pull off the road to sit before the Lord. Receive the Lord's peace and rest before you carry on with your day. You'll be amazed by the uncluttering of your thoughts that God can bring through sitting a short time with Him.

Allow the Holy Spirit to give you what you need to meet your daily demands as you have a personal two-way conversation with Him. You'll find with God at the wheel, your day will be much more productive, restful, and peaceful!

> Yes, my soul, find rest in God; my hope comes from him. (Psalm 62:5 NIV)

> Now may the Lord of peace himself give you peace at all times and in every way. The Lord be with all of you. (2 Thessalonians 3:16 NIV)

Who Do You Trust? 

There are many boats with different purposes. A boat can be small to very large, carry one person or many, and they can look plain to being very elaborate. When you get on a boat, you trust that it will keep you afloat. If you find out that your boat has small holes in the bottom of it, it will eventually sink regardless of how large it is or how good it looks.

The God of heaven is a holy God, and in Him, there is no imperfection or darkness. He is not only your Savior and Lord, He is your friend, and you can totally trust Him in whatever you might face. Allow the Lord to intervene in your situation, for He doesn't want you to sink but desires that you rise up by the power of the Holy Spirit.

In those times when you're feeling overwhelmed and can barely keep your head above water, God knows what you need. You can depend on Him for His counsel and might to keep you afloat even during the most trying times. Spend some time in the Lord's presence, trusting Him to give you everything you need to tackle any challenge that comes along.

Trust in the Lord with all your heart and lean not on your own understanding; in all your ways submit to him, and he will make your paths straight. (Proverbs 3:5–6 NIV)

But blessed is the one who trusts in the Lord,
whose confidence is in him. They will be like a
tree planted by the water that sends out its roots
by the stream. It does not fear when heat comes;
its leaves are always green. It has no worries in
a year of drought and never fails to bear fruit.
(Jeremiah 17:7–8 NIV)

Loved Beyond Measure 

> *Then you will be empowered to discover what every holy one experiences—the great magnitude of the astonishing love of Christ in all its dimensions. How deeply intimate and far-reaching is his love! How enduring and inclusive it is! Endless love beyond measurement that transcends our understanding—this extravagant love pours into you until you are filled to overflowing with the fullness of God!*
> —Ephesians 3:18–19 TPT

Whenever you arrive at a certain destination in your life, there is always a starting place. God has a plan for you, but it takes small steps of faith—trusting in Him and putting one foot in front of the other to get there.

God wants to be the ultimate spiritual destination of your heart. He wants to be the one that you seek to find each day. When you take time to enjoy His presence, you'll find true peace and fulfillment that you could never find without Him. God said, *I have come that you might have life.* Not just any life but to absolutely know that you're loved beyond measure. When you keep your focus on Him and listen to His voice, He will give you guidance, strength, and wisdom that will continually build your faith and bring you encouragement.

Explore the destination areas that the Lord wants to take you being willing to open the door and walk through to the other side. The Lord still has much for you to see and experience while you're here on earth. Allow Him to direct you, bring you peace, hope, joy, and give you abundant life!

> Because your love is better than life, my lips will glorify you. (Psalm 63:3 NIV)

Though the mountains be shaken and the hills be removed, yet my unfailing love for you will not be shaken nor my covenant of peace be removed, says the Lord, who has compassion on you. (Isaiah 54:10 NIV)

House of Mirrors 

> *Every good and perfect gift is from above, coming down from the Father of the heavenly lights, who does not change like shifting shadows.*
> —James 1:17 NIV

Have you ever gone into a fun house and looked at yourself in the mirrors and they distort what you look like? One mirror makes you look short and wide, and another mirror makes you look tall and skinny.

In this world, one might not see or encounter many attributes in others that reflect the loving character of God. Therefore, it can bring to one's mind a distorted perspective of who God is. God is loving and holy and sees all things clearly and perfectly without shifting shadows. God's heart is pure, thinking only of your good. You can trust in Him to give you the clarity you need when the answers to certain circumstances are difficult to find.

God is the father of good gifts, let Him begin to show you the way He sees things from a godly point of view. Then your outlook of your circumstances through the eyes of Jesus will not be confusing but will bring light, knowledge, and understanding that has no distortion or shifting shadows.

> For God, who said, "Let light shine out of darkness," made his light shine in our hearts to give us the light of the knowledge of God's glory displayed in the face of Christ. (2 Corinthians 4:6 NIV)

> For I know the plans I have for you, declares the LORD, plans to prosper you and not to harm you, plans to give you hope and a future. (Jeremiah 29:11 NIV)

Difficult Conversations 

> *Let your conversation be always full of grace, seasoned with salt, so that you may know how to answer everyone.*
>
> —Colossians 4:6 NIV

Have you ever heard the expression, "The ball is in your court?" Alluding to the fact that it's the other person's turn to make a move which can be an action or a conversation that might be desired or expected.

When conversations in relationships become difficult and awkward and you'd rather avoid them than have a confrontation, take it to Jesus. He will bring to your mind what you'll need to help you get that approach shot to the other side of a needed conversation without fear of losing points with someone you care about.

God cares about everything that concerns you. In any relationship that might be a struggle whether it's a necessary conversation or an action the other person might expect, openly share with God all that's on your heart. He will give you wisdom and a strategy on what your next play should be, giving you that needed advantage!

> Be completely humble and gentle; be patient, bearing with one another in love. Make every effort to keep the unity of the Spirit through the bond of peace. (Ephesians 4:2–3 NIV)
>
> Do not let any unwholesome talk come out of your mouths, but only what is helpful for building others up according to their needs, that it may benefit those who listen. (Ephesians 4:29 NIV)

The Sparrow

So don't be afraid; you are worth more than many sparrows.

—Matthew 10:31 NIV

It's interesting that when a sparrow lays eggs, incubation is by both parents. When the eggs hatch, both parents also feed the nestlings sharing in their care. Most human parents that have children want to give good gifts to their kids. They feed and clothe them, give them love and affirmation, and teach them in many different ways during their youth and beyond.

As caring parents, siblings, aunts, uncles, and grandparents, anxiousness can arise if something negative happens to one we love or care about. If a family member has an accident, loses a job, or has health issues, you might ask yourself, do I really trust God to get my loved one through this circumstance?

You'll discover that God can be trusted with the smallest to the very big things in your life and in the lives of your children and those you love. Bring all your concerns to the Lord because He cares for you. As you know, God feeds the sparrow, yet you are much more valuable than the birds of the air!

> And my God will meet all your needs according to the riches of His glory in Christ Jesus. (Philippians 4:19 NIV)

> If you say, "The LORD is my refuge," and you make the Most High your dwelling, no harm will overtake you, no disaster will come near your tent. For he will command his angels concerning you to guard you in all your ways. (Psalm 91:9-11 NIV)

Barriers of the Heart 

A happy heart makes the face cheerful, but heart-ache crushes the spirit.

> —Proverbs 15:13 NIV

When breaking the shell of a walnut, it's usually easier to use a nutcracker. As you put pressure on the shell, it begins to crack, and parts of the shell will begin to break off. When you pull away enough of the shell, you can take out the edible nut and enjoy it.

Perhaps you have experienced certain things in your life that have wounded you, and knowingly or unknowingly, you put up an outer shell or barrier around your heart. God might use a little pressure in your circumstances to begin to crack and break off areas of that barrier that you've built up. His desire is to bring healing to you and for your heart to remain soft and pliable in His hands.

When you get hurt by others, don't put up a sign that says, "Do not enter." Be willing to forgive and release them to the Lord. He doesn't want you to harden your heart and carry that pain. As your barriers slowly come down, continue to walk forward with God. You'll find your heart will begin to soften, and you'll find total freedom in your life that only Jesus can bring!

> I will give you a new heart and put a new spirit in you; I will remove from you your heart of stone and give you a heart of flesh. (Ezekiel 36:26 NIV)

> Now the Lord is the Spirit, and where the Spirit of the Lord is, there is freedom. (2 Corinthians 3:17 NIV)

Rays of Light

Every good and perfect gift is from above, coming down from the Father of the heavenly lights, who does not change like shifting shadows.
> —James 1:17 NIV

Although it may be cold and cloudy outside, Jesus is the light that shines throughout your day. He surrounds you with the warmth of His presence and brings you peace and rest. He reveals Himself to you daily in unexpected places and in different ways that you don't necessarily notice.

God might reveal Himself to you through a bright smile from one you love or hearing a songbird greet you as you rise for the day. When meeting a good friend for lunch, you reccive a warm hug and a bouquet of flowers from them. If you're taking a few days off and going out of town, you enjoy the beauty of God's creation all around you as you drive to your destination. These might be small things, but they bring rays of light to your day making a powerful impact.

God is good every day, and it's easy to take some of these blessings for granted. Look for His rays of light that He shines upon you each day and thank Him for the beauty that you enjoy through those you love and through His awesome creation.

When Jesus spoke again to the people, he said, "I am the light of the world. Whoever follows me will never walk in darkness, but will have the light of life." (John 8:12 NIV)

This is the message we have heard from him and declare to you: God is light; in him there is no darkness at all. (1 John 1:5 NIV)

Stay in Alignment with Jesus 

> *For I know the plans I have for you, declares the*
> *LORD, plans to prosper you and not to harm you,*
> *plans to give you hope and a future.*
> —Jeremiah 29:11 NIV

If you're in a hurry and ignoring what condition the asphalt is in as you're driving, you may come upon a large pothole quickly. When your tires run over it, you can possibly do some damage to your alignment and your tires.

There are times when coming in contact with a pothole in life brings awareness to something you cannot see or are not paying attention to. Do not always avoid or swerve around an issue that God wants you to go through when steering through situations in life. There are lessons of growth that God wants to teach you by going through them.

Stay in alignment with Jesus by having an attitude of thankfulness. Bring everything before Him in prayer when you hit a circumstance that you didn't see coming and don't understand. The wind of the Spirit will give you what you need to handle the road before you, and God will lead and guide you in the direction that will drive you toward your destiny.

> Rejoice always, pray continually, give thanks in
> all circumstances; for this is God's will for you
> in Christ Jesus. (1 Thessalonians 5:16–18 NIV)

> Suddenly a sound like the blowing of a violent
> wind came from heaven and filled the whole
> house where they were sitting. (Acts 2:2 NIV)

Personal Canvas

As you begin to paint a picture, you can see in your mind what you would like your picture to look like when it's completed. Mixing the right colors and using the right size and type of brush help to bring your painting to life. Painting a picture is a process, and your spiritual growth is also a process and takes time.

As you spend time in God's presence and in prayer, ask what He wants you to focus on in the season of life you're currently in. Like a mural on a wall, there are times God might want to draw your attention to the bigger picture in a particular circumstance. Trust Him to help you make wise choices when making decisions. Other times, He might target the fine details He has placed in front of you to possibly bring correction or bring small changes to improve a situation.

As you walk daily with Jesus in every season, He will cover your personal canvas with spectacular beauty and joy that is life-giving to you. Put your trust in Jesus, for *He who began a good work in you will carry it on to completion!*

> I praise you, for I am fearfully and wonderfully made. Wonderful are your works; my soul knows it very well. (Psalm 139:14 NIV)

> For we are His workmanship, created in Christ Jesus for good works, which God hath before ordained that we should walk in them. (Ephesians 2:10 KJV)

Finding the Good

> —1 Chronicles 16:34 NIV

Many of God's people are looking closely at the trouble and pain that's happening in the world. They are focusing their attention on wickedness, destruction, death, and loss. Don't give too much time and attention pondering what Satan is doing. Negative talk about everything from political issues to family problems can open doors to depression, anxiety, fear, discouragement, and disillusionment.

Even though it's not reported on national television or seen with your own eyes, God is accomplishing great things all around you every day! Miracles of God are always taking place. People all over this earth are being saved, healed, and made whole. He is continually providing, protecting, and bringing provision to those in need.

Don't allow the enemy to steal your joy and strength, but turn your attention to the majesty of Jesus. Look to the good that He's accomplishing every day in your life and in the life of your family. Replace negative talk with thankfulness for all that God has done, all He is doing, and continuing to do!

> Always giving thanks to God the Father for everything, in the name of our Lord Jesus Christ. (Ephesians 5:20 NIV)

> Do not be anxious about anything, but in every situation, by prayer and petition, with thanksgiving, present your requests to God. (Philippians 4:6 NIV)

Let's Communicate

My sheep listen to my voice; I know them, and they follow me.

—John 10:27 NIV

Communication is a very important aspect of everyday life. You communicate with your family, friends, coworkers, those you see at church, and others that participate in activities you are involved in. There are many ways to communicate with people today, face-to-face, phone calls, email, texting, FaceTime, Zoom, and through social media.

However, God longs to communicate with you in the realm of the Spirit. As you come into the presence of God, He communicates to you like no other. God's agape love for you is pure, gracious, unconditional, and immeasurable. He is always seeking the good for your life, bringing encouragement, comfort, joy, hope, and peace.

As you come before the Lord and call out His name, you can be assured that your call will not go unanswered. God is ever present with you, and He knows every thought you think and every word you're going to speak. He is able to answer every question you have because His wisdom is limitless. Communicate with Jesus and let Him bring rest to your mind and heart.

> The Lord replied, "My Presence will go with you, and I will give you rest." (Exodus 33:14 NIV)

> You discern my going out and my lying down; you are familiar with all my ways. Before a word is on my tongue you, LORD, know it completely. (Psalm 139: 3–4 NIV)

Book of Life

Your word is a lamp for my feet, a light on my path.
—Psalm 119:105 NIV

Have you ever been looking for a book to read but have not been able to find it? A library is full of all kinds of books: fiction, nonfiction, mysteries, poems, children's books, cookbooks, and how-to-books, to name a few. Unlike the West where the outlaw gets what's coming to him and that's the end of the story, God's book, the Holy Bible, is alive! It is powerful and sharper than any two-edged sword, and even though it is very old, it makes personal application for your life today. It does not die out or fade away as the years go by, and it adds to your personal arsenal with each chapter that you read again and again.

God has spoken through men by the power of the Holy Spirit to write the words contained in the Bible. God loves you, and He wants to drench you with His words of life. There is so much that He wants to say to you each day. God wants to fill your heart with joy, peace, hope, and wisdom that is contained within its pages.

Take advantage of this book of life that God has given to you. Open it daily and let the Lord speak to you. It holds God's promises and personal application that you need day-to-day. It is truly a *lamp for your feet and a light on your path!*

> Then he taught me, and he said to me, Take hold of my words with all your heart; keep my commands, and you will live. Get wisdom, get understanding; do not forget my words or turn away from them. (Proverbs 4:4–5 NIV)

May the God of hope fill you with all joy and
peace as you trust in him, so that you may overflow with hope by the power of the Holy Spirit.
(Romans 15:13 NIV)

Passage

Take delight in the Lord, and he will give you the desires of your heart.

—Psalm 37:4 NIV

You envision taking that next step going forward in your life that you feel God is directing you toward, but you don't have all the answers of how to go about getting there. You may have a heart's desire to pursue missionary work in another country, knowing you are called, but don't have the finances. Or perhaps you may be taking a new direction in business, but you don't have certain connections that you need to get started.

When the plans you desire are part of God's will and purposes for your life, He will become the bridge that you need allowing you to cross over to the other side. God will provide passage for you leaving the old and entering the new. He will help you to overcome obstacles and avoid any detours that tries to prevent your progress.

Surrender any uncertainty to God. For He knows what you have need of, and He will lay out the answers before you as you require them. Rest in His presence, trust in Him, and He will encourage you, give you direction and hope, and envelop you in His love and peace.

> And we know that in all things God works for the good of those who love him, who have been called according to his purpose. (Romans 8:28 NIV)

> Now may the Lord of peace himself give you peace at all times and in every way. The Lord be with all of you. (2 Thessalonians 3:16 NIV)

Wondrous Creation 

> *God blessed them and said to them, "Be fruitful and increase in number, fill the earth and subdue it. Rule over the fish of the sea and the birds in the sky and over every living creature that moves on the ground."*
>
> —Genesis 1:28 NIV

The hummingbird is small but mighty. Don't judge its small stature as being insignificant. The hummingbird can beat its wings so fast that it makes a humming sound beating an average of seventy-five beats per second. The hummingbird is one of God's special creations. When people look upon it, they wonder, *How does that bird do that?*

God creates so many beautiful things that your eyes look upon. When the seasons change and the snow falls, it becomes a majestic white wonderland. In springtime, the flowers are beautiful when they are in full bloom delivering a wonderful fragrance that fills the air. In the summer, spectacular sunsets that paint the sky as they hang over the oceans make the end of your day picture-perfect.

When in the midst of your daily busy schedule, you might not always notice the beauty of God that surrounds you. However, God's beauty is always before you, and He's created it for your enjoyment. Thank Him for the beauty of the mountains, stars, and beaches as well as in the small intricate details of His creation such as the wings of a hummingbird!

> In his hand are the depths of the earth, and the mountain peaks belong to him. The sea is his, for he made it, and his hands formed the dry land. (Psalm 95:4–5 NIV)

How many are your works, Lord! In wisdom you made them all; the earth is full of your creatures. There is sea, vast and spacious, teeming with creatures beyond number—living things both large and small. (Psalm 104:24–25 NIV)

Life-Giving Springs

I will refresh the weary and satisfy the faint.
—Jeremiah 31:25 NIV

Do you at times feel like you are standing on sand dunes where all you see is hot dry sand in every direction and you don't know which way to turn? God knows there will be times in your life when you feel distant and dry spiritually, and that is not what He has for you. When you find yourself in that desert place, cry out to Jesus because He's always listening for your voice, waiting for you to ask Him for help and guidance.

Jesus will give you peace and take you to His heavenly oasis where you can rest and drink from the life-giving springs of the Holy Spirit. You will be refreshed; He will order your steps daily and place you on the right path.

As you call out to Jesus and fix your eyes on Him, you won't enter that desert place, but instead, you'll bask in the oasis of His Spirit that never fails, for it is always bubbling up to meet you!

> The LORD is my shepherd, I lack nothing. He makes me lie down in green pastures, he leads me beside quiet waters, he refreshes my soul. He guides me along the right paths for his name's sake. (Psalm 23:1–3 NIV)

> On the last and greatest day of the festival, Jesus stood and said in a loud voice, "Let anyone who is thirsty come to me and drink. Whoever believes in me, as Scripture has said, rivers of living water will flow from within them." (John 7:37–38 NIV)

An Everlasting Love 

God's everlasting love for you is like the waves of the sea—continual, powerful, yet peaceful. There is no end to the deep love God has for you. As your mind thinks upon the height and depth of His love, the reality is, you have only touched the surface. Your mind cannot begin to fathom the vastness of God's eternal unconditional love for you.

When you feel you're doing well, do you feel God loves you more or you're more deserving of His love? When you know you've fallen short, do you feel that God loves you a little less? The truth is that nothing can separate you from the love of God because His love isn't based on your performance but on who He is. God is love.

God's love is unconditional, constant, devoted, tender, compassionate, and the love He bestows upon you is everlasting!

> For I am convinced that neither death nor life, neither angels nor demons, neither the present nor the future, nor any powers, neither height nor depth, nor anything else in all creation, will be able to separate us from the love of God that is in Christ Jesus our Lord. (Romans 8:38–39 NIV)

> May be able to comprehend with all saints what is the breadth, and length, and depth, and height; And to know the love of Christ, which passeth knowledge, that ye might be filled with all the fullness of God. (Ephesians 3:18–19 KJV)

Rocket Up

> *Have I not commanded you? Be strong and coura-geous. Do not be afraid; do not be discouraged, for the LORD your God will be with you wherever you go.*
>
> —Joshua 1:9 NIV

As a rocket goes up in space, there is excitement for those outside of the spacecraft that are working and those that are watching. The astronauts inside the spacecraft are probably a little nervous and excited as they listen to the countdown. If it's their first time in space, they will now have an opportunity to see what they have never seen before. The unknown becomes a first-time experience that they take on with eyes wide open as they see up close the beauty of this universe that God has created.

Going into unknown places and situations here on earth that you've never experienced before can be a little frightening at times. It can also open your eyes to what's possible and can help you learn and grow every time you step into a new and perhaps challenging circumstance.

Allow God's love to fill you and lift you higher into the spiritual atmosphere, for there is so much more for you to see in the light of His awesome presence. God's glory fills the universe. Don't stay too earthbound, but experience supernatural joy as you skyrocket closer to the King of kings and Lord of lords in heavenly places!

> Jesus looked at them and said, "With man this is impossible, but with God all things are possible." (Matthew 19:26 NIV)

Then the Spirit lifted me up and brought me into
the inner court, and the glory of the LORD filled
the temple. (Ezekiel 43:5 NIV)

Letting Go 

Trust in the Lord with all your heart lean not on your own understanding; in all your ways submit to him, and he will make straight your paths.
— Proverbs 3:5–6 NIV

Now perhaps you've been involved in certain groups and ministries for a long time, and now God is asking you to let go of them and move forward with Him as He has new assignments for you. However, you're having difficulty letting go because you've become familiar and comfortable over the years with friends and tasks, and you haven't reached that point where you've wanted to let go. You're also concerned that new future changes might not be as satisfying as what you're involved in now.

Hold on to the hand of Jesus and ask Him to help you take that next step in your life that He desires for you. When you let go and let God direct you, He will not let you fall, but He will put you on the path that is right for you in each season of life.

Letting go of what's familiar is not always easy, but trust in Jesus as He will give you the strength to move forward. His plans for you are always good. Let Him guide you with peace, and see what opens up before you!

Forget the former things; do not dwell on the past. See, I am doing a new thing! Now it springs up; do you not perceive it? I am making a way in the wilderness and streams in the wasteland. (Isaiah 43:18–19 NIV)

Thou wilt keep him in perfect peace, whose mind is stayed on thee: because he trusteth in thee. (Isaiah 26:3 KJV)

Treasured Possession 

For you are a people holy to the LORD your God. The LORD your God has chosen you out of all the peoples on the face of the earth to be his people, his treasured possession.

—Deuteronomy 7:6 NIV

Although the Lord has blessed you with many good gifts in your life, there has been some disappointments, discouragements, and loss that you have encountered. During this season, your life is not experiencing the abundant blessings you've hoped for.

When you come before God and sit in His presence and his glory surrounds you, it is there that you can be filled to overflowing by the power of the Holy Spirit. He is all that you need as His treasure is always abundant, and He longs to be your supply every day. You'll find His treasure chest is always full of love, rest, peace, wisdom, knowledge, understanding, and joy.

Look into His eyes and come face-to-face with Jesus, and let any disappointment and discouragement dissipate. Look to Him, follow Him, and hold on to his hand, for He loves you and longs to fill every need that you have. Allow Him to show you the precious jewel that you are in His eyes. He desires to be your personal treasure that brings you encouragement, refreshment, mercy, and compassion overflowing!

But you are a chosen people, a royal priesthood, a holy nation, God's special possession, that you may declare the praises of him who called you out of darkness into his wonderful light. (1 Peter 2:9 NIV)

My goal is that they may be encouraged in heart and united in love, so that they may have the full riches of complete understanding, in order that they may know the mystery of God, namely, Christ, in whom are hidden all the treasures of wisdom and knowledge. (Colossians 2:2–3 NIV)

Walking Out the Journey 

*For I know the plans I have for you, declares the
LORD, plans to prosper you and not to harm you,
plans to give you hope and a future.*
                                    —Jeremiah 29:11 NIV

You have spent many years on your education, sometimes staying
up all night trying to finish your papers and long reports by the
deadline. Reading what seemed like countless books, rehearsing slide
shows, and giving speeches in front of the class. When you completed your education, you did get hired and started working at what
you thought was your dream job. However, after being there awhile,
you realize it's not going in the direction you hoped it would, and
you are having regrets about accepting this position.

You begin calling out to God in prayer, He hears your cry and sees
that discouragement and disappointment is weighing heavy on your
heart. Keep your gaze upon Jesus, and at the appointed time, He will
direct your paths and open the door that He has prepared for you to
walk through. Do not be anxious while waiting during this time of
transition. He will give you what you need daily to go forward peace-
fully and joyfully by the power of the Holy Spirit.

Walk out this journey with Jesus one step at a time as the place you're
currently in is a temporary one. Stay close to Him as you wait for
Him to open the right doors of opportunity and connections. Jesus
loves you, and He *knows the plans He has for you, plans to give you a
hope and a future!*

> Do not be anxious about anything, but in every
> situation, by prayer and petition, with thanksgiv-
> ing, present your requests to God. And the peace
> of God, which transcends all understanding, will

guard your hearts and your minds in Christ Jesus.
(Philippians 4:6–7 NIV)

The LORD himself goes before you and will be
with you; he will never leave you nor forsake
you. Do not be afraid; do not be discouraged.
(Deuteronomy 31:8 NIV)

Crumbling Walls

> *Finally, be strong in the Lord and in his mighty power. Put on the full armor of God, so that you can take your stand against the devil's schemes. For our struggle is not against flesh and blood, but against the rulers, against the authorities, against the powers of this dark world and against the spiritual forces of evil in the heavenly realms.*
>
> —Ephesians 6:10–12. NIV

There are walls that exist you cannot see such as someone that builds an invisible barrier around themselves for protection and might choose to close off from others to keep from being hurt. Perhaps you have been hurt by a friend, family member, or someone in the church that did not choose to treat you in a loving way, or you experienced a situation that you felt was unfair. Although you might not admit it out loud, you have put up a wall between you and God because of what happened.

Do not come into agreement with the lies that the enemy speaks to you knowing that he wants to keep walls up that separate the sweet communion between you and God. Although you were hurt and things did not turn out as you hoped, how will you choose to respond?

God is always a good father. Walls bring separation; however, God has created you to walk in joy and freedom. For *where the Spirit of the Lord is, there is freedom!* Tear down any walls by surrendering the past, releasing the pain and disappointment to Jesus, and be willing to forgive. As the walls begin to crumble, move forward in God with joy, strength, and total freedom!

See to it that no one falls short of God's grace; that no root of resentment springs up and causes trouble, and by it many be defiled. (Hebrews 12:15 AMP)

Now the Lord is the Spirit, and where the Spirit of the Lord is, there is freedom. (2 Corinthians 3:17 NIV)

Incomparable

> *For just as each of us has one body with many members, and these members do not all have the same function, so in Christ we, though many, form one body, and each member belongs to all the others.*
>
> —Romans 12:4–5 NIV

Although the tail of an airplane is a relatively small part in comparison to its size, it plays a big part in the plane's stability. Perhaps you feel you are a small part of the body of Christ; however, each part is important and essential. God has called each of His children to use the gifts and talents He's given each one, joining together to serve and encourage those that know Jesus as well as those that do not.

Because of your uniqueness, don't spend time comparing yourself to others. Whether you're a person that's very visible or working behind the scenes, we all need one another.

Jesus is a personal God, and He knows the number of hairs on your head. His loving thoughts toward you outnumber the sand. As you begin to use the gifts God has given you, you'll have a big impact in bringing that special part of who you are to the body of Christ as only you can!

> Each of you should use whatever gift you have received to serve others, as faithful stewards of God's grace in its various forms. If anyone speaks, they should do so as one who speaks the very words of God. If anyone serves, they should do so with the strength God provides, so that in all things God may be praised through Jesus Christ.

To him be the glory and the power forever and
ever. Amen. (1 Peter 4:10–11 NIV)

Now you are the body of Christ, and each one
of you is a part of it. (1 Corinthians 12:27 NIV)

All Who Are Thirsty 

*Come, all you who are thirsty, come to the waters;
and you who have no money, come, buy and eat!
Come, buy wine and milk without money and
without cost.*

—Isaiah 55:1 NIV

When you choose to eat in a cafeteria, you usually do so because of the convenience of its location or because your friends are eating there and you want to spend a little time with them. Unfortunately, the down sides are, the line can be long and slow; they can have a poor selection, and the food doesn't always taste that good.

The good news is that the food and drink that God offers will never end, and they will satisfy your soul eternally. No payment is needed because He has already paid the price for you with His blood when He died on the cross, was buried, and rose again on the third day!

Come into the presence of the Lord and spend time with Him. He sees your weariness and wants to lift off the day-to-day fatigue. Not only does God offer the free gift of salvation but also as you commune and sup with Him, it won't resemble a cafeteria experience. It will be peaceful, restful, and satisfying, filling you with His presence and bringing you refreshment.

For he satisfies the thirsty and fills the hungry
with good things. (Psalm 107:9 NIV)

Behold, I stand at the door and knock: if any man
hear my voice, and open the door, I will come in
to him, and will sup with him, and he with me.
(Revelation 3:20 KJV)

God-Pleaser

How much thought do you give to pleasing man? Your boss, coworkers, family, friends? Perhaps you're working toward a promotion, putting in many hours at work and performing well. However, the boss is not recognizing your efforts, and you're starting to feel discouraged, wondering what else you can do to please him?

People, in general, in our society have a tendency to base success on performance not only at work but also in a myriad of ways. You can get in the habit of pleasing man daily whether you recognize it or not.

However, as your relationship with Jesus gets stronger, your viewpoint and daily focus becomes more and more directed toward Him. You then find yourself wanting to please Jesus rather than man. To please man is earthly, but to please God is eternal. So *whatever you're doing, work at it with all your heart as unto the Lord, for you will receive an inheritance from the Lord as a reward!*

> Am I now trying to win the approval of human beings, or of God? Or am I trying to please people? If I were still trying to please people, I would not be a servant of Christ. (Galatians 1:10 NIV)

> And whatever you do, whether in word or deed, do it all in the name of the Lord Jesus, giving thanks to God the Father through him. (Colossians 3:17 NIV)

Set Apart by Design

For we are his workmanship, created in Christ Jesus unto good works, which God hath before ordained that we should walk in them.

—Ephesians 2:10 KJV

You are like a vivid and striking work of art set apart for God's design. Colorful brushwork details your style and is framed by God's hand creating the masterpiece that you are.

Your work of art is centered and balanced in Jesus, and He holds you upright. Like a priceless painting, you are irreplaceable to Him. There are times you may start to tilt if you become too anxious about a situation by trying to fix or control something in your own strength without inviting God into your circumstance.

It is His desire to fill you with His peace and give you daily direction. Surrender to God and trust in Him to lead you every day. Do not spend your energy focusing on the problem, but turn toward God to bring the solution that is needed. You are His handiwork, His masterpiece, and He holds the palette of wisdom, understanding, knowledge, creativity, counsel, and might!

> And the spirit of the LORD shall rest upon him, the Spirit of wisdom and understanding, the spirit of counsel and might, the Spirit of knowledge and of the fear of the LORD. (Isaiah 11:2 KJV)

> I have filled him with the Spirit of God in wisdom and skill, in understanding and intelligence, in knowledge, and in all kinds of craftsmanship. (Exodus 31:3 AMP)

Safe Path

Every now and then, a change of scenery is needed. Getting away
from work and the city to surrounding yourself in the landscape of
majestic mountains and cool refreshing streams is both welcoming
and relaxing. However, if you begin hiking in an unfamiliar terri-
tory, it's a good idea to be prepared should you run into unfavorable
weather, face a dangerous animal, or lose your way.

When you find yourself in the midst of new or unfamiliar circumstances in your life that becomes overwhelming and you are uncer-
tain of the way ahead, stay close to Jesus. He will order your steps on
a daily basis. Like a dangerous animal in the wilderness, the enemy is
always looking for ways to catch you off guard and trip you up.

Your confident trust is in God alone. He will continually immerse
you with His love and protection. You will not lose your way as He
is the stepping stone that will provide a safe path for you to follow.
He will remove any dangerous rocks along the way getting you to
higher ground.

> But let all who take refuge in you be glad; let
> them ever sing for joy. Spread your protection
> over them, that those who love your name may
> rejoice in you. (Psalm 5:11 NIV)

> Trust in the LORD with all your heart and lean
> not on your own understanding; in all your ways
> submit to him, and he will make your paths
> straight. (Proverbs 3:5–6 NIV)

Brokenhearted 

The Lord is close to the brokenhearted and saves those who are crushed in spirit.
—Psalm 34:18 NIV

God knows the times when you are hurting, and your pain does not escape Him. You may have lost your spouse of many years, and now you don't know how to continue by yourself because you lived life together for so long. Perhaps you've experienced divorce, and you feel the pain of betrayal but have no understanding of what went wrong. Possibly one of your parents or a loved one died in an accident, and like a tsunami that hits suddenly, you feel as though you are drowning in a sea of loss and loneliness.

Even though you cannot see God, He is the God of all comfort, and He is right beside you. He uses other people in your life at specific times to bring encouragement and console you. As a loved one puts their arms around you during a time of need, God's love is also found in their embrace. At God's prompting, a friend comes over to share a meal to cheer you up and to spend quality time with you. Someone you care about calls you at just the right time and speaks words of encouragement and hope to you when you're feeling down.

Look up! For God is the bright sunshine that breaks through your window when you feel the darkness over you finally starting to fade. His endless love and compassion for you brings restoration and healing to your heart!

> Praise be to the God and Father of our Lord Jesus
> Christ, the Father of compassion and the God of
> all comfort, who comforts us in all our troubles,
> so that we can comfort those in any trouble with

the comfort we ourselves receive from God. (2 Corinthians 1:3–4 NIV)

Though the mountains be shaken and the hills be removed, yet my unfailing love for you will not be shaken nor my covenant of peace be removed, says the LORD, who has compassion on you. (Isaiah 54:10 NIV)

Revolving Door

The Lord makes firm the steps of the one who delights in him; though he may stumble, he will not fall, for the LORD upholds him with his hand.
—Psalm 37:23–24 NIV

If you push a revolving door as you enter a restaurant, you would keep going in circles if you didn't make the decision to either step inside the restaurant or back outside. There are times in life you might feel as though you're going in circles. Having no clear direction and asking yourself, Do I step into this, should I step out, or do I stay in a place of indecision that keeps me continually in a place of going nowhere?

When you lack direction, give everything that's on your heart to God in prayer. If things don't become perfectly clear, take a risk and step out in faith in the direction you think God's leading. As you do, He will guide you and give you the clarity that is needed day-to-day, one step at a time.

Trust God to lead your life and place you on the paths of His choosing. Come out of that place of indecision, stepping out of that revolving door, and step into all that God has for you!

> I will instruct you and teach you in the way you should go; I will counsel you with my loving eye on you. (Psalm 32:8 NIV)

> The Lord himself goes before you and will be with you; he will never leave nor forsake you. Do not be afraid; do not be discouraged. (Deuteronomy 31:8 NIV)

Depth of God's Love 

> *For I am convinced that neither death nor life, neither angels nor demons, neither the present nor the future, nor any powers, neither height nor depth, nor anything else in all creation, will be able to separate us from the love of God that is in Christ Jesus our Lord.*
>
> —Romans 8:38–39 NIV

A goldfish living in a transparent bowl can only experience what their small space allows. However, not only can a much larger aquarium that's wider and deeper hold more than one variety of fish but also they'll enjoy a larger area to swim with more width and depth.

God is not limited by space or time, and the depth of His love for you is undeniable and unfathomable. As the Holy Spirit reveals to you the beauty of God's character, dive deeper in the things of the Spirit by entering into God's presence. Worship Him and learn from Him as He teaches you in the Word.

Begin to expand your knowledge and understanding of who God is. Don't stay in a limited space like a goldfish does. God desires for you to participate in a much deeper relationship with Him that consists of so much more than just getting your feet wet. Take the plunge!

> So that Christ may dwell in your hearts through faith. And I pray that you, being rooted and established in love, may have power, together with all the Lord's holy people, to grasp how wide and long and high and deep is the love of Christ. (Ephesians 3:17–18 NIV)

See what great love the Father has lavished on us,
that we should be called children of God! (1 John
3:1A NIV)

Heavy Burden 

*Come to me, all you who are weary and burdened,
and I will give you rest. Take my yoke upon you and
learn from me, for I am gentle and humble in heart,
and you will find rest for your souls. For my yoke is
easy and my burden is light.*
—Matthew 11:28–30 NIV

There probably have been times in your life when you have carried a heavy burden because of certain circumstances that were almost too much to bear. Whether it's a difficult physical task of feeling the weight when having too much work to do or an emotional burden due to carrying guilt or perhaps regretful past events.

Jesus is aware of every part of your life—past, present, and future. He knows exactly how you're feeling in every moment. Because He loves you, He doesn't want you to become weary or carry a heavy burden for any reason.

As you allow the light of His love and healing to shine upon every area of your heart releasing any burden to Him, the heaviness that was weighing you down will begin to lessen. Jesus will take the heavy yoke from you, bearing your burden, and exchanging it for peace and rest.

> So do not fear, for I am with you; do not be dismayed, for I am your God. I will strengthen you and help you; I will uphold you with my righteous right hand. (Isaiah 41:10 NIV)

> Praise be to the Lord, to God our Savior, who daily bears our burdens. Our God is a God who saves; from the Sovereign Lord comes escape from death. (Psalm 68:19–20 NIV)

Change your Garments 

Therefore, if anyone is in Christ, the new creation
has come: The old has gone, the new is here!
                —2 Corinthians 5:17 NIV

The day you came to Jesus and accepted Him as your savior, the Bible says that you became a new creature in Christ. The old things have passed away, and all things are made new. This reality is exciting and gives you a new understanding of who you are in Jesus, exchanging garments of sin for garments of righteousness. However, living in this fallen world, there are times when life is a struggle. Perhaps you find yourself going backward, putting on and wearing a garment of sin or shame, listening to the lies of the enemy and forgetting who you are in Christ.

Jesus came that you might throw off that cloak of sin and shame. He died for you, and His blood covers you. You don't have to walk in that darkness anymore. There is always forgiveness in Jesus, and when you confess your sin, He is faithful to forgive. When the father looks at you, He sees you clothed in the righteousness of Jesus.

Don't get caught up listening to the lies of the enemy that's whispering to you where you fall short. Remind yourself that you are a new creature in Christ, and the Holy Spirit lives within you. You are a child of the Most High God. Walk with Him daily in His righteousness, beauty, majesty, and splendor!

> So if the Son sets you free, you will be free indeed.
> (John 8:36 NIV)

> If we confess our sins, he is faithful and just and will forgive us our sins and purify us from all unrighteousness. (1 John 1:9 NIV)

Calming Rough Waters 

Peace I leave with you; my peace I give you. I do not give to you as the world gives. Do not let your hearts be troubled and do not be afraid.

—John 14:27 NIV

God's disciples enjoyed a one-on-one relationship with Jesus during His ministry on earth. Even so, when traveling on a boat together, a storm suddenly came up, and the waves were so high they swept over the boat. The disciples were afraid because they felt they were going to drown. Jesus calmed the wind and the waves, but He observed their lack of faith.

When the storms of life come, will Jesus find you full of faith? God is with you in every circumstance you face. Will you put your faith in Him and trust that He will help you even when you might feel that the boat you're on is sinking? God's supply is not limited. He will give you everything you need to keep you afloat during the worst of storms.

Keep looking toward Jesus, and do not try to control the situation. As Jesus spoke to the wind and waves and calmed the sea, He will also speak words of peace into your situation, bringing calm over the rough waters that you're experiencing. God is your anchor that keeps you from going adrift in times of trouble. Trust in Him, for His waves of love are always sweeping over you!

May the God of hope fill you with all joy and peace as you trust in him, so that you may overflow with hope by the power of the Holy Spirit. (Romans 15:13 NIV)

Therefore, since we have been justified through faith, we have peace with God through our Lord Jesus Christ. (Romans 5:1 NIV)

93

Hooked

Now most people will tell you that deep-sea fishing is a relaxing activity as well as challenging to the fisherman that loves being out in the open sea. One of the many ways to catch a fish is with colorful lures that can move and spin in such a way that is appealing to fish. The fish will start to chase the lure thinking he is going to get a tasty snack, only to get hooked by the fisherman.

Have you experienced getting lured in, hooked, caught up in, or chase certain things in this life that look really good to you in the moment, but after some time goes by, you realize that it doesn't really satisfy you for long? The things of this earth are temporal and its pleasures fleeting. If you're a child of God, heaven with Jesus will be your eternal home. Only in relationship with Him and being in God's holy presence will you find everlasting love, peace, and joy that does not fade away.

Make the personal choice to walk with Him daily and seek the abundant life only God can bring while on this earth. It's His desire to make you a fisher of men!

> Then He said to them, "Follow Me, and I will make you fishers of men." (Matthew 4:19 NIV)

> I have loved you with an everlasting love; I have drawn you with unfailing kindness. (Jeremiah 31:3 NIV)

Beacon of Light

> *When Jesus spoke again to the people, he said, "I am the light of the world. Whoever follows me will never walk in darkness, but will have the light of life."*
>
> —John 8:12 NIV

A lighthouse tower sits in strategic locations above the waters. It continually shines a beacon of light guiding ships and boats at night as well as warning boats on the sea of dangerous areas so that they will not crash against the rocks.

Will you be God's lighthouse to those in your realm of influence who find themselves in a dark place and have lost their way? He will give you lenses of discernment to be His beacon of light and to bring them rays of hope in the name of Jesus. God's eyes are continually upon those that find themselves unanchored and have gone adrift.

Allow God to use you as His lighthouse revealing His love light to those that are hurting, reminding them that God's never-failing love always surrounds them. He will guide them to the shore of safety and, by the power of His Spirit, will lift them up and enfold them in His protection and peace.

> I will lead the blind by ways they have not known, along unfamiliar paths I will guide them; I will turn the darkness into light before them and make the rough places smooth. These are the things I will do; I will not forsake them. (Isaiah 42:16 NIV)

This is the message we have heard from him and declare to you: God is light; in him there is no darkness at all. (1 John 1:5 NIV)

Distant Heart

> *Do you not know? Have you not heard? The* LORD *is the everlasting God, the Creator of the ends of the earth. He will not grow tired or weary, and his understanding no one can fathom. He gives strength to the weary and increases power of the weak.*
> —Isaiah 40:28–29 NIV

A tornado can bring devastation to an entire community or area without much warning. There is no control over the extreme power of the wind and airborne debris when it starts to head in your direction.

Perhaps there have been unwise decisions made by those close to you in your life. Consequently, you have suffered devastating effects that you had no control over because of those decisions. God is not a God that does not feel or understand. He is not a God that does not see or hear. He has walked alongside of you every moment, and He has felt the sorrow and grief you have gone through.

Because of your brokenness, your heart became distant toward God for a short time. As a loving father, God is wooing and drawing you closer, pouring out His peace and comfort over you. Restore your trust in Him as He is in the process of rebuilding the things that have been broken and stolen. God's steadfast love for you is unstoppable, enduring forever.

> My eyes will watch over them for their good, and I will bring them back to this land. I will build them up and not tear them down; I will plant them and not uproot them. I will give them a heart to know me, that I am the Lord. They will be my people, and I will be their God, for they

will return to me with all their heart. (Jeremiah 24:6–7 NIV)

Give thanks to the LORD, for he is good. His love endures forever. (Psalm 136:1 NIV)

Drenched in the Spirit 

As the waves crash onto the seashore day and night, God wants you to
stay continually drenched in the waves of His embrace and presence.
Allow the refreshment of the Holy Spirit to pour over you bringing a
total calm to your mind and emotions.

God knows that the times you are living in are not only hectic but
also very challenging and difficult. As you focus on what's going on
in the world around you with all its trouble, return your thoughts
toward Jesus and gaze upon Him. Take time to sit in the pool of
His vitality and experience God's joy and peace even in the midst of
swirling chaos that might be happening around you.

Stay drenched in God's refreshment and restoration, and as you continue to put your trust in Him, God will fill you with hope, encouragement, and blessings, leaving any anxiety, fear, or heaviness that
you've been carrying far behind!

> Peace I leave with you; my peace I give to you.
> I do not give to you as the world gives. Do not
> let your hearts be troubled and do not be afraid.
> (John 14:27 NIV)

> May the God of hope fill you with all joy and
> peace as you trust in him, so that you may over-
> flow with hope by the power of the Holy Spirit.
> (Romans 15:13 NIV)

A Forgiving God

The Lord is not slow in keeping his promise, as some understand slowness. Instead, he is patient with you, not wanting anyone to perish, but everyone to come to repentance.

—2 Peter 3:9 NIV

In the story of Jonah, God told him to go to Nineveh and tell the people that if they didn't repent of their wickedness, they would be destroyed. Jonah didn't want God to forgive the Ninevites. He ran away, but Jonah couldn't hide from God. He was swallowed by a big fish and was in the belly of that fish for three days. After the Lord had the fish spit him out, Jonah did obey God and went to Nineveh. The Ninevites believed God, declared a fast, and put on sackcloth and repented. When God saw that they turned from their evil ways, He had compassion on them and did not bring destruction on them. However, Jonah was not happy that God was merciful toward them.

Have you encountered anyone in your life that has hurt you deeply or wronged one of your family members? You might feel that certain people that have done evil don't deserve their sins forgiven. Like Jonah, you might question if they've done anything in their lives to qualify for God's grace. However, anyone that comes to the Lord is not out of reach of God's willingness to forgive and to save. God's desire is that no man should perish. If one gives their heart to the Lord, God can change them from within, and they can become the person God created them to be.

God has forgiven you and will continue to forgive you as you confess your sins during your lifetime. How much more should you forgive those that sin against you? God is love; He is compassionate, forgiving, and merciful to all of those He created in His image.

Bear with each other and forgive one another if any of you has a grievance against someone. Forgive as the Lord forgave you. (Colossians 3:13 NIV)

Because judgment without mercy will be shown to anyone who has not been merciful. Mercy triumphs over judgment. (James 2:13 NIV)

Promises

Let us hold unswervingly to the hope we profess, for he who promised is faithful.

—Hebrews 10:23 NIV

God created the rainbow as a result of His covenant—a promise that He would not destroy mankind again with water. In His Word, God gives many promises to you. He does not want you to skip over His promises but to meditate on, believe in, declare out loud, and to stand on them. God's promises are full of encouragement, power, and hope. God has freely given them to you to use when you need them during your walk with Him in this life.

What are you going through in your life right now? What do you need from God today? Are you in need of healing? Are you dealing with new challenges and need God's strength? Are you fearful? God has given you His powerful promises in His Word.

Whatever you might be facing, do not be disheartened, but walk in the assurance that God's promises are for you now. Begin to speak and declare His powerful promises out loud on a daily basis. You serve a God of abounding grace, hope, compassion, strength and wisdom. Let God's promises uplift your spirit and bring you encouragement, peace, and victory!

> For no matter how many promises God has made, they are "Yes" in Christ. And so through him the "Amen" is spoken by us to the glory of God. (2 Corinthians 1:20 NIV)

But those who hope in the Lord will renew their
strength. They will soar on wings like eagles; they
will run and not grow weary, they will walk and
not be faint. (Isaiah 40:31 NIV)

Flourish

> *The righteous will flourish like a palm tree, they will grow like a cedar of Lebanon; planted in the house of the LORD, they will flourish in the courts of our God. They will still bear fruit in old age, they will stay fresh and green.*
>
> —Psalm 92:12–14 NIV

Have you ever noticed a fruit tree that looks healthy and is flourishing? Its roots go deep into the soil bringing nutrients the tree needs to sustain life. Along with sunshine and water, it begins to thrive, bearing lots of fruit in its season. The fruit of the tree tastes good and imparts refreshment to those that eat from it.

When your relationship with the Lord begins to grow, it can resemble a flourishing tree. As you commune with God, reading the Word, praying, and having fellowship with other believers, your spirit begins to thrive. You become strengthened, unmovable, and unshakable with God by your side.

When you're planted in Him, He will use you for His purposes. Continue to grow in the deep things of God, staying close to Him, and spending time in His presence, and watch the fruit you will bear as you flourish in God!

> But blessed is the one who trusts in the LORD, whose confidence is in him. They will be a tree planted by the water that sends out its roots by the stream. It does not fear when heat comes; its leaves are always green. It has no worries in a year of drought and never fails to bear fruit. (Jeremiah 17:7–8 NIV)

Those who trust in their riches will fall, but the righteous will thrive like a green leaf. (Proverbs 11:28 NIV)

Behind the Scenes

Being confident of this, that he who began a good work in you will carry it on to completion until the day of Christ Jesus.

> —Philippians 1:6 NIV

Do you at times feel like you're moving at a fast pace in your life; however, like walking on a treadmill or riding a stationary bicycle, you know you're moving but don't feel you're getting anywhere?

When it seems that you're doing all the right things to move forward spiritually but are not seeing the desired growth you thought you would see at this stage in your life, you begin to question that something is wrong. Do not get discouraged, for God is always working, although you might lack understanding about what He's doing. He might be in the process of building your character or perhaps He is increasing your faith or preparing you for what lies ahead in the near future.

Stay mindful that God loves you, and His eyes are always upon you. He is always speaking, continually listening, never standing still, but always working for your good behind the scenes in your life!

> And we know that in all things God works for the good of those who love him, who have been called according to his purpose. (Romans 8:28 NIV)

> I will instruct you and teach you in the way you should go; I will counsel you with my loving eye on you. (Psalm 32:8 NIV)

The Power of Words 

Do not let any unwholesome talk come out of your mouths, but only what is helpful for building others up according to their needs, that it may benefit those who listen.

—Ephesians 4:29 NIV

Have you seen a child's face light up when he or she attempts to play a game for the first time and you're close by watching? You're cheering them on whether they win or lose with affirming loving comments, and that brings a huge smile to their face!

Words can have a powerful effect on people. Negative words that are spoken in haste or with a harsh tone can hurt feelings, bring anger, or impart a feeling of worthlessness and defeat. On the other hand, loving and encouraging words that are spoken can uplift, bring joy, and hope to one's heart.

Our God is a God of everlasting love. He speaks to you with words of encouragement when you're not feeling as confident or joyful as you'd like to. Following the example of Jesus, use a friendly tone when speaking to family members, those at work, and people that you meet on a daily basis. Kind and loving words will bring encouragement, confidence, and hope to those that are listening!

A soothing tongue is a tree of life, but a perverse tongue crushes the spirit. (Proverbs 15:4 NIV)

The words of the reckless pierce like swords, but the tongue of the wise brings healing. (Proverbs 12:18 NIV)

About the Author 

Carol Blose lives with her husband and daughter in Southern California. As a follower of Jesus for over thirty-five years, she and her husband have been involved in church leadership and have helped to lead a house church for ten years. They have ministered to the poor, led home groups, gone on short-term missions, and Carol has facilitated women's bible studies and ministered in Healing Rooms. Currently, Carol and her family serve the body of Christ where Jesus leads them in their church and in the community. In addition to writing, she also enjoys expressing herself creatively through painting.

Through her journey, Carol has learned to put her trust in Jesus and be confident in Him. In her past, she has gone through sleepless nights and anxiety trying to control her circumstances. As she began to surrender and release her needs to God, she experienced the goodness of God, His mercy, answered prayer, and the peace and presence of God that comes with living close to Him. Her personal prayer is that every person who reads this book will learn to have a *confident trust* in Jesus.

www.ingramcontent.com/pod-product-compliance
Lightning Source LLC
Chambersburg PA
CBHW022024150726
47990CB00002B/804